WRITER'S INK

Yolanda Wright

Copyright 2022 - Ready Writer, Inc.
All rights reserved.

This book is protected under the copyright laws of the United States of America. This book or any portion thereof may not be reproduced or used in any manner whatsoever - electronic, mechanical, photocopy, recording, or any other - including information storage and retrieval systems, without the express written permission of the publisher, or author, except for brief quotations in printed reviews.

Scriptures marked CJB are taken from the COMPLETE JEWISH BIBLE (CJB): Scripture taken from the COMPLETE JEWISH BIBLE, copyright© 1998 by David H. Stern. Published by Jewish New Testament Publications, Inc.
www.messianicjewish.net/ jntp.
Distributed by Messianic Jewish Resources Int'l.
www.messianicjewish.net. All rights reserved. Used by permission.
Scriptures marked CEB are taken from the Common English Bible, copyright 2011.
All rights reserved. Used by permission.
Scriptures marked AMP are taken from the AMPLIFIED BIBLE (AMP): Scripture taken from the AMPLIFIED® BIBLE, Copyright © 1954, 1958, 1962, 1964, 1965, 1987 by the Lockman Foundation. Used by permission. (www.Lockman.org)
Scriptures marked KJV are taken from the KING JAMES VERSION (KJV): KING JAMES VERSION, public domain.

Published by Ready Writer, Inc.
Buckeye, AZ 85396
Info@areadywriter.org
ISBN 979-8-9853996-2-2
Library of Congress Control Number: TXu002328982

This book is dedicated to my mom, Ruby Mildred Howell, a citizen of heaven. You were such an inspiration in my life. Your strong faith in God and time spent writing will never be forgotten. Thank you for believing in me and sharing in my ministry.

I would like to give a very special thank you to:
My Stylist, Felicia Johnson (felicia.johnson2@outlook.com)
My Makeup Artist, Amy T (Makeup Artistry, LLC)
My Photographer, Tracy Cargo (Tcargo610@gmail.com)

Contents

True Story	1
I Am	2
Beguiled	3
The Fixer	4
The Urge	6
Then, It's Him, Not Me	7
True Story	8
Because I'm His, I Know I'll Be Okay	9
The Winds of Change	10
Today I Cry	11
The Christmas Gift	12
A Conversation with Me	14
You Slipped Away	15
They Walked as Gods	16
The Invited	17
When There Was a Nobody	18
Decide Today	19
They Say I Gotta Move	22
Passion of A Worshipper	24
You are My Gift	26

Be Confident	27
The Encounter	28
Just Be	30
When Sleep Came	31
And So The Story Goes	32
Communing with God in the Still of the Day	34
Ouch! Thorns!	35
Quiet	36
Know This	37
Re-Member-ing	38
Rocky Road	39
Identity Christ IS	40
Saved	41
The Steppers Club...	42
Get Going	43
Come Away With Me	44
If You Only Knew	45
Out Of The Ashes I Rise	47

True Story

I was in the 2nd or 3rd grade, sitting at my desk, feeling a little mischievous that bright, sunny morning. Now, our classroom sat at the end of a long hallway. Well, it sure seemed long to me and the other 25 small, energized, people that sat in my class everyday. At the other end of the hall was the Principal's office. This particular day, there was a knock on our classroom door. My teacher went to answer the knock, which happened to be a parent........ not mine though 🙂. She stepped out of the room for a quick second and returned to say, "Quiet! No talking, I'll be right outside this door." Well, as I said, I was feeling a little mischievous. So, I said to my classmates, "I bet you I'll scream." They looked at me..... you know, THAT look. Then, all of a sudden, out of NOWHERE, a huge, black fly flew around me and flew smack dab into my EAR! Talk about a scream! It resonated, vibrated, and penetrated right through that door. I couldn't help it; I had to scream! Yep! She sure did - my teacher suddenly appeared in the room! I can still see her face, and into the coat closet she sent me to spend my time of punishment. I'm still laughing! Be careful of what you speak! Words are powerful. Everything is listening.

The one who guards his mouth [thinking before he speaks] protects his life; The one who opens his lips wide [and chatters without thinking] comes to ruin."

Proverbs 13:3 AMP

I Am

That I Am
Your God
Your Creator
Your Master
Your Healer
Your Deliverer
Your Prince of Peace
Your Righteousness
Your Sanctifier
Your Victory Banner
Your Joy
Your Strong Tower
Your Way Maker
Your All Sufficient One
Your Comforter

Your Strength
Your Everlasting Father
Your Shepherd
Your Guide
Your Teacher
Your Friend
Your Bread of Life
Your Living Water
Your Protection
Your Anointing
Your Breath of Life
I am Alpha and Omega
The Beginning and The End
I Am
That I Am

Selah

Beguiled

Who told you that you're not loved?
Who told you that you were sick?
Who told you that you were poor?
Who told you that you couldn't?
Who told you that you wouldn't?
Who told you that you'd never be....?

Don't listen to the lie!

The Fixer

I was broken, shattered, torn, hopeless, helpless and worn. People told me about the Fixer who lives not far away, who'll come to your rescue any time of night or day.

They said He'll take you and put you back together. He'll heal your brokenness, and He'll mend your shattered dreams. His specialty is the torn, helpless and worn. He makes all things new, the Fixer.

"Is there really help for me?" I thought to myself as I listened. Then somewhere deep inside of me I got a sense of hope. It was as if a flicker of light glowed within my soul. I thought to myself, "oh can it be, will He really fix me?" I pondered, "Why would He, how could He, Oh would He, the Fixer, fix me?" Thoroughly convinced, what else could I do. I said, "I'll call the One they called the Fixer." Then everyone replied, "He's never let anyone down! He's known all over town! There's no job too great or small. He's the Fixer, can fix it all!" I set out on my journey to find this one they called the Fixer. I searched high and I searched low, and everyone I saw I asked, "The fixer, do you know?" They'd reply, "yes I do, He made me all brand new!"

My desire for Him, the Fixer, grew and grew and grew. "They called Him the Fixer, but what's His real name," I inquired. "His name is Jesus Christ," they replied, and in my heart I cried. I must find the

Fixer, whose name is Jesus Christ. I know He'll make a huge, huge difference in my life. Just get on your knees and pray to Him today. Call upon His name, and He'll answer right away. So in my desperation I knelt down beside a tree and began to call His name, Jesus. "Won't you please help me?" I'd hardly finished my sentence when I felt His presence. A calming sense of peace flooded my entire being as I asked Him to fix me and make me new like He had done for others. "Make me like them, too." I felt instantly forgiven, was overwhelmed by His love. So grateful to have met Him, Jesus Christ, Son of God from above.

Now I understand why the people said He lives not far away. He's living in my heart now, fixing me everyday. I can see and feel the changes.

He's making me all brand new. I wouldn't trade him for anything, cause nothing else will do. So if you're worn, torn, helpless and hopeless, then you need the Fixer too. His name is Jesus Christ, and I'm sure He'll help you, too.

I have His calling card, an invitation to you. It states, "Call upon me, and I will answer morning, noon, or night. No job is too great or small, I'll take care of it all. Just call JESUS, and I'll take care of the rest."

The Urge

To do better
  To be better
    To be the better one
      Won't stop clocking
        Tick tocking
        Tick tocking
      Am rocking, noonday thrills, evening,
    slow down if you will
        Like a power surge, energizing your nerves
      Some can maintain
     Others can't restrain
   The Urge

Then, It's Him, Not Me

When I'm weak, I am then strong
When I am sad, I am then glad
When I am poor, I am then rich
When I am broken, I am then whole
When I am lost, I am then found
When I feel unloved, I am then loved

When I am sick, I am then healed
When I can't see, my eyes then are opened
When I am grief stricken, I am then comforted
When I am worried, I then have peace
When I have nothing, I then have all I need
When I have doubts, I then have faith

When I don't know, I then know all things
When I've sinned and repented, I then am forgiven
When I'm fearful, I am then bold
When I am empty, I then am full
When I am unkind, I then can show mercy
When I am foolish, I then have wisdom

When I don't know, I then have knowledge
When I'm heavy laden and tired, I then have rest
When I feel friendless, I then have a friend
He gives me the power to be everything I'm not!
He is Jesus Christ
All that I Am then He is

True Story

I wrote my first song when I was 5 years old. I can remember it so well. My sisters and I were playing church in my grandmother's bedroom. My oldest sister was playing the tiny, upright piano, and my younger sister was the church. My morning praise song was called Keep Up The Music. And it went like this: Keep up the music, keep up the music, keep up the music, all night long....ohhh keep up the music, keep up the music, keep up the music, all night long.

We sang it over and over and over again. At 5 years old, I didn't have all the words to describe my praise offering to Him, but I had no inhibitions; I gave Him, Jesus, my best. Psalm 66:1-2 says, "make a joyful shout to God all the earth! Sing out the honor of his name; Make His praise glorious."

Don't be dismayed or afraid because of the multitude of things we face in this life. Go forth singing and praising and glorifying God while He fights on your behalf. What's your praise song? Sing it out! Sing it long! Sing until your spirit feels strong. Let the praises of God arise in you today. Let your praise be heard by the One who loves you the most.

Because I'm His, I Know I'll Be Okay

I am not my own. I belong to my Father above.
I've been purchased with the high price of love, paid for with Jesus' blood.
I need Him every day to live this life on earth, through sorrows and pain, hard times, and tear drops like rain.
Knowing that I'm His gives me the strength and courage to keep on going, living, loving, and caring.
Sometimes life is like white water rafting.......... unpredictable, and rough. Tossing and turning, all washed up. The currents of life ever-changing...... and yet because I'm His, I know I'll be okay.
I just turn it over to Him, and He gives me rest. And when I meditate on His goodness, He fills me with joy, peace, and strength.
I'm looking forward to each new day and what it brings because I know I'm His, and I'll be okay.
Beloved now are we the sons of God, and it doth not yet appear what we shall be: but we know that when He shall appear we shall be like Him: for we shall see Him as He is.

The Winds of Change

Soft Summer wind, oh gentle breeze, come whisper upon my world.
Soft Summer wind, gentle breeze, you set my soul at ease.
You're like the calmness of the seas or drifting falling leaves.
My world is at ease because of you.
Don't leave soft Summer wind, oh gentle breeze, be pleased to linger still.
Yet I know that you must go, no doubt you'll return at will.

Stormy wind, gusty turbulent wind, into our lives you blow.
You stir and toss things to flight wherever you're pleased to go.
Sometimes it's necessary to shake and stir things up a bit.
In preparedness we will wait for the time when you will hit.

We can always count on you to come strut your gusty stuff for the swirling, tossing, stirring is good, although it can be tough.
Stormy wind, gusty turbulent wind, you forced us to amend, for the betterment of our lives, is that what you intend?
If this is true, I oblige you, stormy, gusty, turbulent wind.

Today I Cry

Tears for hope that remain
Tears for joy and pain
Tears for sorrows past
Tears for promises kept
Tears for God's mercy and grace
Today I cry
Tears for dreams unmet
Tears for memories I can't forget
Tears for wanting more
of what God has for me
I know Jesus see my tears and hears my heart cry,
and I don't mind at all that He knows my vulnerability
Today I cry
And my tears are safe with Him.

The Christmas Gift

Micheala sprang from her bed in the wee hours of the morning. She ran towards the large picturesque window in her living room. It was the window she so often peered from as a small child. Back then it seemed so huge, as if to dominate that whole side of the room. Micheala would always watch the seasons come and go and wondered, "how did they know, who told them to come and when to go?" Springing from her bed was almost as constant as the season, but this time it was different.

Micheala, while asleep, heard the sound of a still small voice that awakened her. All of her senses were keen so her body responded immediately. But not out of fear or desperation but in wonder and anticipation. As she hurried to the living room window, stumbling over wrapped Christmas presents and toys, she fell among the presents. Micheala let out a screeching whelp. She had fallen many times before but this time it was different from any fall she'd ever had.

As Micheala lay there on the floor she stared at the ceiling while warm tears fell from her eyes. She wondered why her parents had not come to rescue her. "Hadn't they heard her fall," she thought to herself. After all, they usually come quickly to help her. Suddenly Micheala heard that still small voice again, and her thoughts returned to the picture window. She continued to lie still on the floor. As she listened she heard Him say, "I've answered your prayer Micheala look and see!" Micheala's heart began to pound and she sat up as if someone had lifted her up. There she saw one of the most precious gifts, one that she always prayed for. As she moved her gown across her once crooked legs she saw two of the most beautiful perfect legs any person would want! This Christmas her prayer was answered. "Oh thank You, Jesus, thank You, Jesus," she exclaimed! Micheala's joy filled the whole house and everyone came running in to see what all the praising was about. Everybody saw Micheala's new legs and began praising God as well. We worship You God of Israel! We worship You King Of Kings! We worship You because You are faithful and true. And you heard our prayers! You are the reason for the season! There would not be Christmas had it not been for You.

Micheala was 14 years old and a strong believer in Jesus Christ. She remained faithful to believe that God does miracles. She no longer needs the help of her parents and crutches for now her once twisted legs are beautiful and straight. During her high school years Micheala ran track and danced ballet; she was great at both.

The End

A Conversation with Me

I'm feeling great today and strong
Feeling like I can dance all day long.

To music.... good to my soul
a hummmm soothing.... down to my toes
Gonna live today like never before.

I'm fearless, I'm free, and there's no stopping-

I'm me.

You Slipped Away

30 years have come and gone for us; you leave me here to mourn. With so many, many memories, good ones, bad ones, happy and sad ones, too many to go on.

My tears are hot for us, for what could have been. But I mustn't tarry here long for it's not good for me.

Sometimes I feel angry and alone, and that's not fair for you or me. Wow, even in death I consider you, my husband, my friend.

I miss your big, tall frame and that gentle smile you wore so well. I miss those gentle hugs and stories only you could tell.

I miss holding your hand when we walked down the streets. I miss you chasing me through the house and loving it when I'm caught. You truly were a gentle, quiet soul with a heart big enough to have and hold me.

I love you.

They Walked as Gods

They walked as gods in the earth, with power and authority. There was no visible crown or scepter nor robe of dignity.
They walked as gods in the earth, clothed in majesty. They were formed and fashioned by His hands, by God Almighty.
They walked as gods in the earth, giving names to every creature great and small. There was nothing they couldn't do; they had authority over it all.
They walked as gods in the earth, communing with God in the cool of the day. In the still of the day, they talked.
They walked as gods in the earth although under authority. Ye shall not eat of the tree of the knowledge of good and evil, for you shall surely die. These words were spoken by God to them, but they did not comply.
In disregard, they ate of the tree, now dead men walking you see.
Seduced by the enemy of their soul, they believed the lie satan told.
Once clothed in majesty now clothed in fear and shame,
life certainly would not be the same.
They walked as gods in the earth no more because of the sin they bore. Mere humans, stripped of their royalty, they became slaves of their own humanity.
Then Jesus steps down from eternity and embraces the scene as Son of God and King. He gave His life as a sacrifice, an atonement for all, you see.
He shed His blood on Calvary's cross, setting all mankind free.
He restored their position as gods in the earth with power and authority. And now they walk as gods on the earth. Who are they?

They are we.

The Invited

The ordinary in appearance, no special qualities,
no pomp and circumstance or a group of wannabes.
Down trodden and hopeless with dreams deferred
Heads hung low with a voice not heard
Rich and content, knees not bent
Prideful and boastful, greed won't relent
The sick and afflicted, maimed and dejected,
weak and scorned, the outcast, the outclass
Liars, cheaters, adulterers, deceivers,
blasphemers and dreamers, oppressed and distressed
Killers of life, idolaters and thieves, sexually immoral, the filthy, the unclean
Prideful and haughty, boastful, crude, rejected, dejected, oh the multitude
Heavy laden with heartache, sadness, and confusion
Rejected, ostracized, abused and criticized
The fearful and the bold, the young and the old, the rich, the poor
All are invited, as you can see, to live a life with Jesus Christ for all eternity
For God so loved the world that He gave His only begotten Son, that whosoever
believes in Him should not perish, but have everlasting life.
For God did not send His Son into the world to condemn the world, but that the
world thru Him might be saved.

YOU are THE INVITED!

When There Was a Nobody

When there was nobody
Searching high and low for everybody, but nobody could be found.
Nobody searched high and low for Somebody, going to and fro....for somebody.
Does anybody know?
Nobody found Somebody.
Somebody was right there all the while. Nobody had only to open his heart and greet Somebody with a smile.
Now anybody knows everybody needs Somebody in their life.
The One Somebody who's Lord and Savior, His name is Jesus Christ.
So, if you're like nobody, looking for everybody, who's trying to find Somebody, He's already there. Just open your heart and let Him in; you'll never be nobody ever again.

Decide Today

For I know the thoughts that I have toward you, Saith the Lord, thoughts of peace and not evil, to give you an expected end.

Jer. 29:11, KJV

Decide Today
I want what God wants for me, peace and a future filled with hope.

Keep thy heart with all diligence; for out of it are the issues of life.

Prov. 4:23, KJV

Decide Today
I will guard my heart from bitterness, anger, and unforgiveness

And the Lord shall make thee the head and not the tail; and thou shall be above only and not beneath; if that thou harken unto the commandments of the LORD thy God, which I command thee this day, to observe and to do them.

Deut 28:13, KJV

Decide Today
I am a leader. I am successful.
I am above and not beneath.

There is no fear in love, but perfect love casteth out fear: because fear brings torment. He that fears is not made perfect in love.

1 John 4:18, KJV

Decide Today
I am filled with God's love.

I am made perfect in His love.
Fear has no hold on me!

A soft answer turneth away wrath, but grievous words stir up anger.

Proverb 15:1 KJV

Decide Today
I will consider my words before speaking.

Every wise woman builds her house, while the foolish woman tears it down with her own hands.

Proverbs 11:14 CEB

Decide Today
I am building my house.
I'm building on a sure foundation, God's Word.

He who walks with the wise will become wise, but the companion of fools will suffer.

Proverbs 13:20 CJB

Decide Today
I am wise.
I am a great influence on those around me.

Lying lips are an abomination to the Lord, but they that deal truly are His delight.

Prov. 12:22 KJV

Decide Today
I am God's delight. I speak truth.

Give, and it shall be given unto you, good measure, pressed down, and shaken together and running over shall men give into your bosom.

Luke 6:38 KJV

Decide Today
I am a giver.
I look for ways to give.

Those who hear but don't do the word are like those who look at their faces in a mirror. They look at themselves, walk away, and immediately forget what they were like.

James 1:23-24, KJV

Decide Today
I am a ready listener and a doer of God's Word

Now thanks be unto God, which always causes us to triumph in Christ and maketh manifest the savour of his knowledge by us in every place.

2 Cor. 2:14 KJV

Decide Today
I always triumph in Christ.
My life is a sweet aroma to those around me.

Surely goodness and mercy shall follow me all the days of my life: and I will dwell in the house of the Lord forever.

Psalm 23:6, KJV

Decide Today
Goodness and Mercy follows me.

They Say I Gotta Move

Been here for quite some time now.
Living, loving, laughing, and done some hurting too.
Same ole address, same ole walkway; what am I to do?
THEY SAY I GOTTA MOVE

Many mornings kissed by the sunrise, heralding a brand new day,
that special time for coffee and a prayer to pray.
And the sun set in the evenings on my back porch with me
Would embrace me and say, "goodnight, I'll see you tomorrow."
Can you imagine that!
THEY SAY I GOTTA MOVE

Some great times spent in this ole house
Birthday parties, sleepovers, dinners and dancing,
Baby and bridal showers, praising, hugging, and romancing.
A rainbow of memories and love can't you see?
THEY SAY I GOTTA MOVE

Don't think I'm ready yet
Invested so much in you, see
New roofing cause of age, new heater installed too.
Not to mention gutters, What am I to do?
THEY SAY I GOTTA MOVE

New flooring put in cause of wear and tear
All that walking, running, stomping, skating, not to mention the two floods
Took a mighty fine beaten, those floors. Many folk come through my doors.

THEY SAY I GOTTA MOVE

This is day seven, and I've already been kissed by the sun.
Had my coffee and said my prayer in peace, waiting for the movers to come.
Lord! Here they coming up my walkway, I must greet them at my door.
The door that has swung open a least a million times before.
I walked quickly to open the door with a smile on my face,
when a bright light overwhelmed me, I thought I'd lose my gait.
Stretched out in front of me was my walkway paved with gold.
Everything around me was too wondrous to behold.
Just like that! I'm in my new house now. Lord can this be?
I'm looking at my hands and feet, and they sure look good to me.
I can see everything so bright and so clear.
What's that? Oooooh, that song I hear?
This new house is fit for a queen,
nothing like it have I ever seen.

THEY SAID I GOTTA MOVE

WHY WHO WOULD HAVE THOUGHT, ON DAY SEVEN, I'D BE IN MY NEW HOME IN HEAVEN

Passion of A Worshipper

What is my motivation for worship? What is the driving force that causes me to be enveloped in an intimate, emotional, and spiritual giving of myself, far beyond what my words can express? What is it that stirs my heart, my soul, my mind, my spirit….that inspires me to humble myself and bow down with deep adoration and honor for my God, My Lord, and my King?

What is that driving force within me that draws me near to Him, even in my darkest hours, even in the throes of suffering? Finding that I need to know Him more, the call to worship beckons me, beyond how I feel, beyond what I think. It's a call from deep within. God's Spirit calling to my spirit, come, let us commune together. It is the Love of God that draws me, a worshipper, to worship.

Why do I worship? Because love compels me to worship. Love compels me to worship, to obey my God, to worship Him in spirit and in truth. Love causes me to lay aside my wants and desires and do what He wants and desires, to do His will. It is the love of God that draws me, a worshipper, to worship.

Love constrains me to obey, to worship Him in spirit and truth. Love causes me to seek Him early, to worship even in the midnight hour...to worship...just He and I alone.

My passion as a worshipper causes me to compel, invite, beckon, and entreat others to worship at His throne. My love for Him makes me want to dance before Him. My love for Him causes me to lift my hands in praise. My love for Him causes me to leap for joy, twirl around and lift my voice in praise. My love for Him causes me to be still, and silent, in His presence, to hear His voice, to smell His fragrance, to feel His touch. It inspires me to sing a song, write a poem, to preach the Word, to heal the sick, to open blinded eyes, to lift a heavy burden, to cause a smile, to win a soul, to reach the lost and hurting.

What is my motivation for worship, the driving force that causes me to be enveloped in an intimate, emotional, spiritual giving of myself far beyond what my words can express? It is the realization that it is not my love for Him, but it is His great love for me...that's my passion.

You are My Gift

You are my lover
You are my friend
You've stood beside me
Through thick and thin
I'll always love you
I'll place no one above you
You're my gift from the Father above

                    You are my lover
                    You are my friend
                    You are the sunshine that brightens my heart within
                    I'll always be there for you
                    You are my dream come true
                    You are my gift from the Father above

Be Confident

Because you love God you're in the palm of His hand.
There's no better place to be.
Because you love God all things are yours.
He'll give you your heart's desire.
Because you love God He's with you always.
He'll never leave you nor forsake you.
Because you love God peace is yours to keep.
"My peace I give to you," He said. "My peace I leave with you."
Because God loved you, eternal life is yours.
For God so loved the world that He gave his Only begotten Son that whosoever believeth in him should not perish but have everlasting life.
Because God loves you, you don't have to fear.
Perfect love cast out fear.
There is no fear in love.

Be confident that whatever God says or does, it is for your good because He loves you.

>Be confident that because you love Him, He's always for you.

>>Be confident that He is for you. He is for you. He is for you.

The Encounter

Walking down a busy, crowded street can be one of the loneliest places in the world, even with the sound of car horns, the hustle and bustle of people, and laughter and chatter.

I stopped at a huge storefront window to admire an extraordinary display of beautiful shoes. I squealed inside as I thought to myself, "those shoes could make my feet sing and dance. Why those shoes would make me feel like royalty." There was no limit to the styles and colors of those shoes. My toes were wriggling with excitement!

I just stood there in amazement, when I noticed the reflection of a woman in the window, standing next to me. There she stood, gazing at the shoes, taking it all in, as I was. I watched her as she stood, head down, shoulders slouching, hair disheveled, and her clothes worn and torn. "What a contrast to the shoes on display," I thought to myself. She appeared so needy…..so hopeless…. so desperate. I could see she was tired and probably hungry, too.

I pondered as I watched her admiring the shoes. My thoughts began to soar through my mind. Who is this person? She's someone's mother, someone's sister, someone's aunt or maybe grandmother; she's someone's child!

Forgetting the shoes I found myself staring at her and my heart began to race and my stomach burned within me. When suddenly, I felt a warm breeze brush across my face. It seemed to blow away all the uneasiness and worry that I was feeling.

My attention was now drawn away by the sight of a gentleman standing next to me admiring the shoes as well. He spoke to me, and as I turned to look at him his eyes pierced my soul, as though he saw deep inside of me. I backed away slightly and he said to me, "don't be afraid," as he touched my shoulder.

I was overwhelmed by love in that very instant. I wanted to share this with the woman standing next to me but to my dismay she was gone. I desperately wanted to tell her what this love felt like, this joy, this peace. It felt more beautiful than those shoes in the window. I wanted to tell her how my soul felt so healed and complete. I just wanted to share this new wonder, this new hope. Everything about me seemed different.

I suddenly realized that the moment that gentleman touched me the reflection of the woman in the window disappeared because you see, that reflection WAS the image of me.

Just Be

In the moment
  Thankful
    Breathe the fresh air
      Listen to the sounds of nature
        Observe the birds in flight
          Listen to your heartbeat
            Feel the silence
              Count the stars
                Feel the sun's heat
                  Smell the rain
                    Enjoy the raindrops
                      Smell the flowers
                        Appreciate the mountains and hills
                          Enjoy the ocean view, the high and low tides caused by the moon
                            The valleys low and the plains
                              The seasons come and go
                                Enjoy observing the animal kingdom, great and small
                                  Be thankful to God and bless His name because you are part of something great
                                    God created the world just for you
                                      Be in the moment

Just Be

When Sleep Came

When sleep came they went their separate ways.
A place in time, a space not designed, for sharing with
another.
Side by side, they lay to rest, replenish, and heal.
And although they lay next to each other, they
were far far away,
oblivious and peaceful after a long day.
They awoke and greeted each other with
a morning smile,
a hug and maybe some loving just for a little while.
When days are long and sometimes grueling with so
many things to do.
Thank goodness for the rest ahead. Sleep, they look forward
to you.
They went their separate ways, when sleep came.

And So The Story Goes

Jesus was born to die

For us to live is Christ

On a rugged cross He hung, crucified

Our sins yet forgiven if we believe in Him

Bearing the sins and sickness of this world, for the old and the young

Eternal life, a gift to us all

He suffered and cried, "It is finished!" And hung His head and died. He was placed in an unused empty tomb for 3 days, there He lie. But from the tomb He came forth alive with all power and authority.

He has paid the greatest price for you and for me. He shed His blood on Calvary.

He's made us one with our Father in heaven. We're seated in heavenly places in Him. He's crowned in glory, now King of kings and Lord of lords.

He gave us the Holy Spirit who now lives in us. He will lead, guide and teach us, as we live our lives for Him.

Victorious indeed He was, He conquered death and hell. No greater love than this, that a man would give His life for a friend - You and I.

And so the story goes....

Communing with God in the Still of the Day

The still of the day can be any time of the day when we still ourselves and steal away. Steal away from every problem, every circumstance, and every situation that drains our energy and takes away our focus. God said in His word that He would never leave us nor forsake us.

He is always patiently waiting for us and wanting to hear what's on our hearts. Sometimes in the thick of turbulent times we forget that He's there and allow ourselves to be overcome with worry, dread, loneliness and despair. But He has a gentle nudge, a still small voice, a sweet invitation to come unto Him.

I quote Him, "Come unto Me all who are weary and heavy laden, and I will give you rest." He gives us rest for our weary, tired souls. I often find myself trying to do things on my own, but tiring, I realize my frailty and how much I need Him to help me. So, I slow down and talk with my Father God because He's got the answers. In the still of the day He's listening for your voice.

Will you listen for His?

Ouch! Thorns!

Thorns are the cares and worries of this world. Thorns are the deceitfulness of riches! Thorns are desires for things that draw you away from God. They'll wrap your heart and hold it captive, as your life ebbs away.
Rid yourself of thorn's clutches! Rid yourself of its point of pain that so often steal your growth, peace and joy.

Thorns....... They annoy.

Quiet

Misty rain
 Falling leaves
  Falling snow
   A peaceful sleeping baby
   A warm summer breeze
   A feather blowing in the wind
  Candle lite
 A new 430LS Lexus
Dinner cooking in a slow cooker
 Sweet kisses in the moonlight
  A firefly in the night
   Butterflies in flight
   A grandbaby's hug
   A solemn silent prayer
  A love note  floating in the air to its intended

Quiet is priceless

Know This

I am not my own; I belong to Father God above.
I've been purchased with a high price of love,
paid for with His blood.

      I need Him everyday to live this life on earth.
      Through sorrows, pain, teardrops like rain

Knowing that I'm His gives me strength and courage to keep on going, loving living and caring.

  Sometimes life is unpredictable, rough and all washed up in the currents of life, ever changing.
  And yet because I'm His I know I'll be okay.
  Suffering and troubles won't last always.

I am His, and He is mine.

Re-Member-ing

Have you tried it yet?

Bringing the things to mind again, countless numerous memories of God's goodness, mercy, and grace. There's a special place reserved in our mind that actually contains all of those memories. And we can re-call them at will at any given moment. One by one. Some may take a while to re-call because they've been buried so deep in our subconscious mind while others remain conscious. It's so important for our well being to re-member all of God's mercies and blessings because it makes the heart glad and gives life to your soul. Re-member how He brought you through a difficult situation. Re-member how He touched your body and healed you when you were sick. Re-member how He spoke gently to you and wiped away your fears and tears. Re-member how He protected you in dangerous situations. Re-member His warm embrace when you needed comfort. Re-member His still small voice that made you say, "is that you, Lord" as peace flooded your soul. Re-member His voice of correction and direction to you, His beloved. Each day, re-member these accounts and see a great difference in your life. And when asked have you tried it...

Your answer will be YES, I have.

Rocky Road

On this rocky road I travel, in this blazing heat.
This rocky road is foreign to me. I'm accustomed to the street.
I'm loaded with my bags and gear and a hearty feast to eat.
Wearing my wide brimmed hat cause it shields me from the sun. Yet I'm sweating like a waterspout, a summer rain no doubt!

I'm walking not too fast and certainly not too slow.
Never know who I'll meet, someone else on the go.
There are no road signs as far as I can see, so I'll just follow where the road leads in this blazing heat.

But please let me share with you why I'm not in great despair.
Unseen with the natural eye are my feet, a beautiful pair,
Adorned with the gospel of peace and wrapped in God's love.
I've got peace in any situation in life, be it morning, noon or night. I'm dressed for the occasion and ready for the plight.

Identity Christ IS

I am His and He is mine
I am His golden child
I've been washed in the blood of the Lamb
And perfected by His fire

The reflection of Him is me
For in His image I've been made
Oh the glory of Him surrounds me
Because of the price for me, He's paid

When I speak I hear His voice
I speak only His words
Words of joy, peace, hope, and love
Life giving words from above

I am royalty, God's spirit lives in me
I am the apple of His eye
I declare and decree His promises
They are truth; He cannot lie

No more identity crisis for me
Cause I know whose and who I am
I am His golden child
I've been washed in the blood of the lamb

Saved

Completely forgiven
The right to keep living
Washed in Jesus' blood
Once for all He died
Once for all He cried
Father forgive them
For they know not what they do.
He did it for me......He did it for you
Saved from a burning hell
Saved from a life of despair
Saved from total separation from God, who is Love
Saved to spend eternity in heaven above

The Steppers Club...

Stepping out of the old and into the new! Always moving, always in motion! Living, loving, serving, and creating. Listening to the Lord and obeying.

Our steps are ordered by the Lord you see. So come and hang out with us and win the world for Jesus Christ. I promise you won't be disappointed.

We're steppers, serving with humility.

We're crump for Christ, and we know it.

We're anointed. We're bold. We're growing up but not old!

Get Going

God hasn't given us a spirit of fear
a spirit of trepidation, a spirit of speculation.

God hasn't given us a spirit of doubt,
wandering about with a spirit of hesitation, NO!

He has given unto us a spirit of power, a spirit of love, and a sound mind. What we choose to do with it will determine our ability to impact our own lives and the lives of others.

Walking in love will conquer all evil. Exercising the power He's given us will equip us for every occasion. All things are possible for us who believe.

Possess a sound mind. Allow His mind, the mind of Christ, to be yours.
That will determine your next move.
Get going!

Come Away With Me

He whispered in my ear, "come away with me."
It was the gentleness of His voice that stole my heart away.
I responded with eagerness, "come away with you where?"
He whispered in my ear again, "come away with me."
I did, and I've never been happier.

If You Only Knew

If you only know that you are a royal priesthood....
	IF YOU ONLY KNEW

If you only knew that you are more than a conqueror ....
	IF YOU ONLY KNEW

If you only knew that you could do all things through Christ who strengthens you...
	IF YOU ONLY KNEW

If you only knew that He was wounded for your transgressions and the chastisement of your peace was upon Him...
	IF YOU ONLY KNEW

If you only knew that He shall keep you in perfect peace whose mind is stayed on Him...
	IF YOU ONLY KNEW

If you only knew the power of the spoken word of God and there is power of life and death in your tongue....
	IF YOU ONLY KNEW

If you only knew that you were chosen before the foundations of the world....
	IF YOU ONLY KNEW

If you only knew you were seated in heavenly places in Christ Jesus...
	IF YOU ONLY KNEW

If you only knew that you could call those things that aren't as though they were...
                    IF YOU ONLY KNEW

If you only knew that without faith it is impossible to please God...
                    IF YOU ONLY KNEW

If you only knew that just by asking you could receive the gift of the Holy Spirit and receive boldness to witness...
                    IF YOU ONLY KNEW

If you only knew that you walk by faith and not by sight...
                    IF YOU ONLY KNEW

If you only knew just how much you are loved, just how special you really are....
                    IF YOU ONLY KNEW

If you only knew you were created in His image and He knew you before you were formed in your mother's womb...
                    IF YOU ONLY KNEW

If you only knew that God so loved you that He gave His only begotten Son to die for you so that you could have eternal life...IF YOU ONLY KNEW how true God's word is, you wouldn't be so blue.

                    IF YOU ONLY KNEW

Out Of The Ashes I Rise

I rise from the ashes of the fire that's designed to refine.
It leaves the old unwanted character behind.

In those ashes are the memories of pain, anguish, sorrows, and despair.

In those ashes are flaws, doubts, and fears.
In those ashes are dreams deferred, disappointments, and endless tears.

In those ashes are unforgiveness, bitterness, hatred, and insecurity.
In those ashes are everything you don't want to be.

I rise from the ashes of the fire that reveals who you are now;
Transformed, like being reborn, all brand new,
I rise.
I rise from the ashes of the fire with determination and a new desire,
a desire to be all that He wants me to be.
All that He's freed me to be.

I rise from the ashes aglow like gold. His glory shines upon me.

His strength and anointing empowers me. To walk, talk, and imitate Him as His dear child, I rise.

I rise from the ashes to change the world around me...to be a flame, a light,
To help someone else to see their need for the fire that refines, that gives new life sublime.

When He died, crucified on Calvary's cross and in 3 days He rose from the dead with all power in His hands, truly nothing could withstand.
I rise because He did.

CPSIA information can be obtained
at www.ICGtesting.com
Printed in the USA
LVHW070150121022
730516LV00020B/1201